THE MONUMENT CYCLES

THE MONUMENT CYCLES

Mariner Janes

*To Michael —
To indecency — to
the streets + barricades
erected there — to you!
— with love —*

Talonbooks

Talonbooks
P.O. Box 2076, Vancouver, British Columbia V6B 3S3
www.talonbooks.com

Typeset in Frutiger Serif
Printed and bound in Canada on 100% post-consumer recycled paper
Cover and interior design by Typesmith

Cover image: Detail of the sculpture *El Anatsui, Between Earth and Heaven*
© Rebecca Schear (Creative Commons License 2.0) via Flickr

Japanese text translation courtesy Rachel Enomoto

First printing: 2013

The publisher gratefully acknowledges the financial support of the Canada
Council for the Arts, the Government of Canada through the Canada Book
Fund and the Province of British Columbia through the British Columbia Arts
Council and the Book Publishing Tax Credit for our publishing activities.

LIBRARY AND ARCHIVES CANADA CATALOGUING IN PUBLICATION

Janes, Mariner, 1977–
    The monument cycles / Mariner Janes.

Poems.
Issued also in electronic format.
ISBN 978-0-88922-751-4

    I. Title.

PS8619.A6754M66 2013   C811'.6   C2013-900156-5

for bud
for my wife
for adrian
for all the other susans

face to face with history

khwaykhway, or, new skin

first nations once wrapped their dead
and placed them on raised platforms
offering the corpse of the one who had passed
to sky, to wind and rain
perhaps it is best then
that we offer these captured moments
in the same way
project them across the southeast sky
(why let history keep these? they are our moments
this is our tapestry
she has no right to them
the concrete of the streets here
carries pieces of ash from the great fire
like a scar that reminds you
of your foolishness)
an attempt, maybe, to resurrect
these moments, a refusal to let them
be only "archival material"
like history in the movies
always a dusty tome to be consulted
no, we shout these moments across the now
push them back into our bloodstream
make ourselves new masks, new khwaykhway
with moments for eyeholes
to look out at the burning world

angelic deference

grasp me in these arms i dont care if youre the wrong angel or whatever horrible cause you fight for i dont believe in carry me backwards away icantstand this detritus this pile of junk history i dont want it i disown it cant be me dont tell me i fought for this cause or that i quit where im going i wont need these bullets these rations this compass help me take my clothes off

i dont believe you are who you say how can there be angels for such a horrible cause as victory washing your wings with tears with blood blood i gave it now they cast me in bronze

they never asked how i felt about it

sarah before i left she asked me she was standing weeping in front of her mirror what i thought going to war might change could i really save anyone could i really change the world i thought no but maybe i can change a street corner in front of a train station

maybe if i stand still and stare hard into their eyes theyll see theres no such thing as victory as win-win as the crush of history swells in my broken eyelids i start to get a little dizzy i felt so light there limp-wristed up and backwards now

i dont think i finished what i started

a poem of absence

    this is not a poem
    it is a monument
        it stands in a real place, at a real time
        3:47, in an alley near main and hastings
        you may know it
    the words "kill pigs"
    inked in blue spray
    near the black dumpster
        this monument is here
        because the street and parks are all taken up
        with dead soldiers and famous people
        and besides
        the alley is the place where things fall
        by the wayside
  we have refused an inscription
    but if we had one
    it would read:

THIS IS FOR ALL THOSE
WHO FELL BY THE WAYSIDE

    it would be for all the things
    they never make monuments for

        for susan, who watched her friend pick
        up her last customer
        in this very alley

    for the coast salish
    waiting to greet josé maría narvaez
    as he steered towards what he could never know
    would become a city
    a place for refracting the light of history
    a vortex
        for all the things our cultures bring together

for fibre-optic cables we buried
so we can talk to other cities
and other susans

      for bud osborn throwing his hundred-block rock
      out over the rooftops of the V6A

this monument is specially designed to yell "love! love! love!"
to the people who only pass by
staring at their watches
who refuse to acknowledge this intersection
of pain and wastings
as a part of their city
and the history we bury
beneath it

tekahionwake and the case of the missing muse

oh emily p i'm sorry i
know you never wanted this
no monuments, please, you asked but
here we are, tekahionwake
in this little grove in the park
hidden from the light
a small altar
to smoke out the ghosts
a small testament to hear the song
your paddle sings
rainwater weeping across your eyes
as you gaze east
as we try to explain you to the world
your mother, fleeing her constricting father
in ohio, met your father, the mohawk chief
of the six nations reserve
as if this duality was not enough
you chose to recite half the poems
in your mother's dress
and the others in buckskin
your grandfather's huron
scalp at your side

this history, we demand
be read in two tongues

                              with albino eyes, one grey
                    searching out the shadows your blood knows
                        the absences, the never-coming herd
                           one blue, shakespeare dripping
                              off the edges of your paddle
                    looking west, to where the sky-line melts
                              from the russet into blue

and between these two worlds
in the fog between sea and sky

your feathers float
to find themselves

and us

the geography of memory

luna and clio dance with dandelions in the granite sunshine

a student at l'école polytechnique
a year after the massacre was asked
how the atmosphere was at the school
on this important day
"what he did," she says
"that doesn't affect us"
maybe she is right but
maybe also
this is why we build things like monuments
so that we never forget
that it does affect us
and always will
(and maybe, even, we need it to)
pockets in the centre of the benches, vulva-shaped
catch the blossoms from the nearby cherry trees
and rainwater
and tears
dandelions spring up
in the centre of this circle this moon this womanshape
regardless of their effects on us

the dead poet looks over coal harbour

i: when fated to despair

    when dawn closes in
    on yr serene face
    knee bent wistful
    i know you're already awake

    in fact, hardly slept
    awake in the briny sun facing south

    what are you thinking
    as you survey the too-new city skyline?
    what smoke and wood from what lowland vista
    informs your thought?
    what love holds the breath in your heart?
    and all that bird shit
    really, must have you thinking
    get away from me, ya goddamn pigeon

ii: address to the devil

tell me, old friend, old fiend
old slobbering demon with fingers curled and bleeding,
to where is my soul aim'd upon death?
to which steamy hellhole?
for my tears are pil'd,
and my step is heavy with sorrow and guilt
so when you have done your worst,
scalped and scalded this poor wretch,
and poured whiskey over my head
what hell shall not taste like heaven?
what gale brought your tooth and grin
to bear on my misfortune?

indeed, what man does not know your name
what man has not seen you spilt like sour pus
under weathered and dark lamppost gutters?
or smelled your throat
breathing in the festering wind?
but when my friend threw rocks at the coyote,
he scuttled away into the worn night,
though we knew he had stood a moment before.
and though i know
you're waiting for the moment i slip up and slip
into your grasp
i'll cheat you yet,

but till then, old friend, i wish you well
and to hell and all things so lovely, a kind regard.

time will eat itself (entropy gets the upper hand wrestling jacob)

      the orca leaps from between two moored yachts
      landing stranded behind me
      terrified and desperate
      her giant eyes wheel about
      the salt water gleaming on her rubbery skin
      i decide to talk her to lastsleep and tell
      stories of the past of the place she finds herself
      i tell her of

      the hum of a cessna's engine, winding towards the inlet
      that in 1907 they carried banners around chinatown:
                     stand for a white canada

      fir, cedar, spruce, pine
      radio waving
      dragon boats

                       names and names and names:

        morton, changen, kawayquitlam, hailstone, galiano, lonsdale, salsbury,
               odlum, oppenheimer, dieppe and back and back

      all the way to adam to lightning-maker to first water first sun
      toronto was first "tkaronto"
            where there are trees standing in the water

      the totems watching from the opposite shore
      cedar sentinel of the nuu-chah-nulth
      the invisible cannonball of the nine o'clock gun whirling past
         craigellachie
                the great crush of the thunderbird, descending
                              and, finally
              in the moments before she stops struggling

i tell her of what she has brought here
our mental voids need collective memories
etching into the tree rings
each counting backwards out of the centrifuge

                              denkmal für gedanken
counting time counting unpatience
counting the spaces
                    between thoughts between time
                    marking the palimpsest of memory

experiment in form #44

hijacked at the gates
crescendo for nothing
for lunch there was dim sum
for dinner despair
a two-piece of the like you never saw

ginsberg and kissinger argue in a late-night supermarket bomb bay, or,
political power comes through the barrel of a sunflower

> political satire became obsolete when kissinger
> was awarded the nobel peace prize.
>
> – TOM LEHRER

what thots i had of you, henry kissinger, for i
walked under an atomic sky in silent alleys
with a headache self-conscious, looking at the angry moon.
in my angry fatigues, and shopping for images,
i went into the neon supermarket, dreaming of your conspiracies!
what obfuscations, what pomegranates! whole nuclear families
shopping at night! aisles full of chilean dictators! mercenaries in the
avocadoes, hand grenades in the tomatoes! and you, allende, what
were you doing down by the bananas?
i saw you, kissinger, hateful, lonely old bastard,
poking among the corpses in the refrigerator, and eyeing
the cambodian grocery boys.
i heard you asking questions of each: who killed capitalists?
what price human life? are you my antichrist?
i wandered in and out of the brilliant stacks of cruise missiles
following you, and followed in my imagination by the c.i.a.
where are we going, kissinger? the doors close in
an hour. where does your gun point tonight?
        (i touch your ears and dream of our fight in the
supermarket and feel forlorn)
will we stroll dreaming of the lost america of love,
past green tanks in driveways, home to our oval office?
ah, dear horn-rims, lonely old assassin,
what america did you have when charon quit poling his ferry
and you got out on the smoking aisles and stood watching
the floor of the supermarket yawn wide, and
the watermelon bombs disappear into the black sky beneath?

experiment in form #124 (found poem)

> lenny we lived together in prince george for two years we had
> two kids please find us i know we haven't talked in years i'm
> here in vancouver now talk to frog he knows how to find us

the ambassador

i represent a city called death
steam rises out of the bones
tombs crawl languished through breakfast restaurant

i represent a city called security
i will not hold your hand through the training exercises
if you have questions about the relocation of your business/
belongings/family, they may be put in writing and mailed to:
under the gun
449 great northern way
shockingly good news.

i represent a city called handcuffs
called in face down and muffled
seize us, seize us, please help us
this is an SOS
52 nautical miles north by northwest.

i represent a city called transnational
here today, here today
never left.
you'll need a rifle to find the flashlight.

i represent a city called bright lights
powered by the grip of the labour forces
and held out like a candle to the ocean
there is blood and sawdust
and no one swims under any milky blaze.

i represent a city called home
where refugees cling to a notion
of a notion of citizenship
that waves through changing political winds.
the hunger that day will not kill you
that's not how hunger works.
staring at my toes and thinking of a full hot meal

                                                              in a safe place.

    i represent a city called whirlpool
    where dreams are liquified and spun
    where organs are crushed and turned into a paste for bread
    where bureaucrats sharpen public knives
    and the dawn congeals into a soft drink.

                                        i represent a city called anchor
                                              where the call of duty
                                    is nothing but a civic nod and a bagel

    i represent a city called trust
    where lovemaking is the real deal, man
    where nothing but taxes
    comes between us

experiment in form #191 (paralytic)

    waterfall in the snow
    black coat and jeans
    and that dead frost
    stiff with sparrow

in a station of the metropolis

i.

    slice
    shadowtrack

    bloodlit and luminous

    veering patience
    among impatience

    program
    scheduled
    maintenance
    populace

    i
    many
    i

    gutted
    franchise
    apocryphal
    disambiguation

    careful lines of bird crap
    homefront delineation

    ping-pong brain
    here, but wired into
    another world

    floodlit and vacuous

ii.

notes crawl
out of the underground
penetrate the silence
of the escalators
a haunting little ditty
composed of absence
and silicone

iii.

coming and going
the dawn looks set to crash out
wishful thinking here

alone in the place
an apparition of pound
on the tracks, wet, black

iv.

off the train and walking
but the shipwreck loomed in the corridor
right in my path
prow jutting out of concrete
with a gorgeous woman
erupting out of the bow
no way around
left only to gape
and wonder what
is happening to me

v.

daypulse and anxious
the rhythm of the station
like electronic blood
unwired and surge
flit and blip   flit and blip   flit and blip
engaged and tangled
closing in
pulsing out

nuclear atom bomb   nuclear atom bomb
uclear atom bomb   nuclear atom bom
clear atom bomb   nuclear atom bo
lear atom bomb   nuclear atom b
ear atom bomb   nuclear atom
ar atom bomb   nuclear ato
r atom bomb   nuclear at
atom bomb   nuclear a
tom bomb   nuclear
om bomb   nuclea
m bomb   nucle
bomb   nucl
omb   nuc
mb   nu
b   n

rendering

a swelling, nationalist theme
a commercial being shot in the back
a hole, matches
a purse with a bible, bug repellent, and a .38
a hiroshige hung next to a drowned woman

nails, rope and a screwdriver piled up together
a canvas sack, determined that that's what's best,
no matter what the nature of it
backspaced, delete delete to starting line

from "re: form"

contrapuntal

<pre>
even though time is   lines into themselves
perhaps a human   and into the garden
   invention i can only see myself   of memory
      as moving through it   some plants dead
      i crawled, time passed, i walked   others dying
            cells multiplied, recapitulated   displaced
      social ontology, trumpets   vagueness and greeny
         deoxyribonucleic acid software   wanted only to
   turning hard   hold that
i feel one but   weathered hand
   perhaps am   and strange ribs
   many i own seven pairs of shoes   close to
   am a different person in each   my chest
      pair my blood moves at different speeds   and say
         carries the many cells and voices   sotto voce
         to scream in different corridors   here i'm
            exhausted, in the end, alone   here
</pre>

first sunflower for frost

when i was nine   before the spring had come
my father planted a yard full of
sunflowers   all stalks and bright lids
we planted them beside the garage to grow
with me   and my brothers and sister

and all that summer they grew
and august   found them taller than anyone
october we lit fireworks at their base
and watched the roman candles seemingly spit
out by their yellow mouths   like they were yelling
light at the sky   and for a joke i stood on a crate
in the middle pretending to hang myself
from the clothesline   no one found it funny

then the white frosts crept back   i could see
their giant heads droop   towards the earth
and nothing would satisfy   or save them

my father never understood   any more than me
as we gazed   at the mouldering crop
since then i've never been convinced
that the line could hold   or that my love could break it

experiment in form #183

and empires
and handouts
and folding in on itself
standing
spaced in and outsourced
with no fission defaulted
not my problem
christ not this morning
the heat bloom the little cuts and miracular insulation with her blood vessels all
bursting in her face like   embarrassed fireworks
unsure of usury, or potential thereof

notes towards a poem of impossibility

i.

    past
    genetic drift
    past love songs
    entendres and doubles
    its history, but i wasn't involved.

ii.

    this is the place
    where memory fails,
    if it could ever reach.
    this is not closure.

iii.

    this
    is where language and memory
    cannot fathom, where
    re-membrance is simply a
    sonar blip, a bat's impression
    of distance across a canyon

iv.

      to summon from the sandy depths
      dust, water, unfiltered and impossible.
      this is the task, the want,
      murky as truth.

v.

      the desire for a single voice
      to compose a single tale
      the impossible nature of the task
      of telling memory
      brutal, visceral tap dance, the emptiness
      of light and its simultaneous possibility.

experiment in form #723

the horse's hooves *clove the brazen earth*
mountains closing in
the split the thunder
then came the rain

rain	came	then
a	a	h
i	m	e
n	e	n

shakes the puddles
drops coursing down roofs
huddled in fear

huddled	in	fear
u	n	e
d		a
d		r
l		
e		
d		

tents to the tracks, or,
THE MILITANT MOTHERS OF RAY-CAM

in the dreams of the mothers,
train whistles, macabre
tracks blood-soaked and steel-screaming
footweary and hell-bent for change

BLOCKADING MOMS REJECT CASH

Eight women from the Raymur Place housing project blocked the rail
crossing all day Wednesday.
They were protesting a breach by CNR of an agreement not to move
trains through the crossing until after 3:45 p.m., because their
children have to use the tracks going to and from school.

it was 1971
it was frustration and anger
it was tents suddenly sprung up
on the tracks, wet and cold

They wore signs reading: "Petitions don't work," "Save our kids,"
"Children before profit" and "Tragedy before action?"

in the dreams of the mothers
smoke, cages and bureaucracy
rail lines tied into ouroboros
lauchlan hamilton's face, laughing

Raymur Place mothers say they turned down a $1,000 offer to end
their protest blockade Wednesday at the Pender Street train crossing.

in the dreams of the mothers,
eyes up
trackshine
promise and future
fury and patience

*At about 9:15 a.m. a CNR train, ringing its bell and steadily sounding
its whistle, attempted to cross the intersection but came to a halt in
front of three rows of women and children.*

and so it began –
the last great train holdup
in canadian history

tents to the tracks
mothers to the rails

*"We turned down the money," said Mrs. Judy Stainsby. "We are not
playing games.*

["MILITANT MOTHERS ... all-night vigil kept by lamplight"]

cover of the *georgia straight* may 14–18 1971: six children holding
up a sign with a drawing of the crossing, saying

"Practice what you preach –
put safety
first."

                                        the railway heads
                                        gave the mothers a sheet
                        that showed they would restrict train times

*Said Mrs. Sheila Turgeon of 527 Raymur:
"That paper doesn't mean nothing."*

                                        breath cold in the night
                                        lamplight and ferocity
                                        and a will unbending
                                        we ain't takin' no shit

[the first CPR locomotive
to arrive in vancouver
came by sea]

though perhaps
no one could see it coming:

MILITANT MOTHERS WIN FIGHT AGAINST RAILWAY

TWO RAILWAYS MAKE DEAL WITH MOTHERS
We won, we won,

after this victory, another:

RAYMUR TENANTS FIGHT FOR CENTRE

*Almost 700 of the 1,200 tenants are children and many parents don't
like their youngsters to roam far from the project.*

then came the demand for a community centre
        a heart to be constructed
        joined into the arteries
        of the neighbourhood
        into the veins
        of the tenants
        the junkies
        the working moms who needed child care
        the elderly
        the poor
        the lonely
        the children
        the pushed-around
        the helpless

it was 1972
it was hope and community
the ray-cam co-operative centre
was born

trains to passing

    forwards to nowheres
    equally as delicious as the salmon, baked
    halved and barbecuing
    the sharp tongue of the flesh
    a warm respite from the cold

    we change vistas as often as minds
    either prairies or vast sums of apartments
    subdivided, retracted, in traction
    tangible in an intangible sense

vanishing point

> Pedestrian motor functions ... create one of those "true systems
> whose existence actually makes the city."
>
> – MICHEL DE CERTEAU

map making
exclusive use
newspaper box
penthouse suite
huddling for warmth
tactile
uniform

> *spatial practices in fact secretly structure the determining*
> *conditions of social life*

definition
anomaly
institution
pre-eminent
dilated pupils crack cataract
panoptician
gentle
kingly
familiar

> and the underpass was the only cover

aberration
walk it off
deal
deal with it
deal with it until tomorrow
no phoenix and gutbusted
all the plans fell apart

> even emily won't talk to me anymore, my own goddamn sister

fumigate
contradiction
political technology
coffee the only saviour
differentiate
city's common practitioners dwell
hallmarked for destruction
understanding eludes us
geographic
coat and boot comprehension
hair slicked back with grease
temporary arrangement
leprous apparently

> *urban life allows what has been excluded from it by*
> *the urbanistic plan to increase even further*

tracks and paths
trains and veins
melodrama
gridded
influx
cunning and stubborn
management network
derail
epic struggled
systems analyst
space maker
rationalization
ground level
old converse behind the fire escape
discipline
bread
controlled operations
uncontrolled utterances

The relics of meaning, and sometimes their shells, the inverted
leftovers of great ambitions, maybe for walking

outside the sphere
invisible
fragmentation
bracketed
clean space
transgression
structure of a myth
stylish interiors
red blanket
coded tranmission
four-inch blade
gaps, slips and allusions
symbolism
furniture
encounter

city of dust

stolen in like rumbles beneath the eyes
less likely to kiss than to fondle
grave, unexpected joy
bearable, not fuzzy
cigar, lunch, banking

it was a joseph conrad moment

sweating it in, rather
no toil equals no blissly sums
the other great use of sawdust
is that it soaks up blood so easily

she rose like a tangent wind
and just pried me open
she never looked back
except for that one time

got a new tattoo; unconvinced but
wishing i could believe in my own thoughts

clock ticking, an unconvincing cliché
but accurate nonetheless
time in
time out
coagulation of the thought

repetition, the best sense of it
and the worst
counting windows or beans
acrylic, dipping toilets into paint mixture

but even when time should be yours
in your mind; if your body cannot be
a single line of thought is hard to sustain
in the din
and the schlurping sucking sound of the paint vat
calling to me like oblivion in a black dress

is it wrong to consider death for myself
so close to the wake of a death here beside me?
is it *only human*

tasteless, like strychnine or gas bills

cleo and me

snakefisted, eyelinered, she clutched at my
raspy throat, we strolled together
so lonely, in the end, on the dirt roads
sandals unfrayed, the edges of her
long dress laced with sorrow and lapis lazuli
we peered over the edge of the temple roof, watching her
self watch the people so far below, so ants, so far gone
a hisssssssss slipped from my lips, her hips pursed and then parted
she cursed the gods but made love to them in her sleep
the bees came and breathed so heavy i couldn't stand
the sunlight was breaking into my scalp, i thought i
was less than, was not enough for her for her
i would have raised
the dead

false witness (language part one)

    home amongst the guns, the snug fit of barrel
    into holster, no sense of timing, i'm told

        lifted the shirt off the rack and thought
        oooooooo that crisp smell

a day in the life of excerpts
version 1.23.27

            graves as far as i could see
                but in the most eloquent language of space
      only a lot of money could explain it

          i looked down at the view, the sharp angle
                away from the deck and thought
      what a fall
      that would be

                  the particular sound
            a hand makes on linoleum really got to me
                and i couldn't get over it

rubbed lotion into hands from a sample jar
at the mall
smelled like death
and flowers all day

undulated (language part two)

with the city in his veins
with the discount sale in hand
no verge of, or otherwise

lighter in pocket, spinning it
on a disc of nervousness
i had no idea how he did it every day

slipped sessions, snuck out, singing sin songs, singing gin,
snaking and sliding along sorry so

cup full of nothing, today, not overbrimmed or pasteurized
not by default, social circumstance or credit loan alike
not housed or not held, not purchased either
no elevator, but an empty shaft, a buzzer on each floor

rinsed out, septically speaking
she wore a black scarf and had the looks of
persephone, or some other snowbird

kearnel

i!
i am!
i am trying!
i am trying to come!
i am trying to come to terms!
i am trying to come to terms with the world!
i am trying to come to terms with the world and my place in it!
i am trying to come to terms with the world!
i am trying to come to terms!
i am trying to come!
i am trying!
i am!
i!

approach

we all seem to approach, perpetually
on the move, destinationed
influxed, mercurial, trajectoried, moving in
wards or out, but the instrument
the effect
the closing
the new distance, the new knowledge of space
(which is always becoming new), lingering only briefly
in each zone
an account of the self usually includes motion:
i'm going home i'm heading out i'm going inside it's cold head
first and foremosted, fluxing and frosty kins
hip, heaving head up and forward
waves and waves, radiation and electricity, washing
clean out but never clean. particularity
and pleasance to each a station, in motion
temporarily, spatially
transit is the destination
measure for measured breaths, clocking in
and counting down town
arterial and batteried, ipodded and slackjawed
hypothesis or veritable institution? where
to begin i might have written in motion, or
tried to catch just one i in the crowd
but it is hard to see the eyes as a one
in the many
any movement is movement in a system
systematically includes continuity and franchised
bucking no stars, no meaning in no place, so
it is the task to stand a part, to norm
to accidental nowhere, and just get there
reflective, each route does not reflect its opposite
but we're on it anyway
horizontal and tilting, suicidal slowdowns only, please
condition on parade and move in the making
start with starting, finish over and over

in the shangri-la

Vance was fresh back from detox and did too big a smash and he decided to clean his paintbrushes with thinner and he lit a smoke started a fire that set his vinyl raincoat on fire fast and he tried to get out his window but he fell backwards out of it and went one storey down and a planter broke his fall and man my heart was beating like boom boom boom and I thought for sure his back was broken but it turns out he was just fine but man he didn't make any friends that night Roger and I took turns kicking his door booting it and booting it until the frame gave way and the water from the sprinkler pipes flooded out in to the hallway like a burst ocean or heart.

Kyle carried the biggest sword I'd ever seen down the stairs and said, "I'm going to kill him. I'm going to cut his head off. I will not stop trying to kill him everytime I see him until me or him is dead. Period. And you can't stop me."

Shaved the plastic from the wires for hours and hours, started at 3:27 a.m. and went till 1:23 p.m. Took the copper, left the shavings on the sidewalk where he'd cut them, and sold it to the scrap metal guys. They always paid less than it was worth, but how was a junkie to argue with cash from wire that he'd lifted from a construction site that same night? Cash is cash. Took the money, got a hit from T., went to his room and did it by himself. Woke up two hours later, got straight back to work binning and collecting bottles and scrap metal. "My god, if he was this hardworking in banking or something ..."

Sarah wept and wept, I never knew what for. Her thin thin frame raked by use and tears, guilt, malnutrition or no food at all for days, cockroaches running the show. It got so bad you felt like you needed to ask the cockroaches permission to enter, a cockroach passport. Her tears piled up and up, frantic with this debt or that, this trick gone wrong, this john owes her that, this one way to get through a bitch of a day followed by that cunt of a day, was she pushed down the stairs or fell I guess. Broken arm didn't slow her down in the least. Hit in the face with a board a month later. Face purple like a starfish. She was like a knot or a windstorm; the worse she was treated the stronger she got.

Sam hustled from the moment of his waking to the time that he never went back to sleep. Seemed to anticipate every word I might say, full of problems, unwanted solutions, terse and always gutwrenched. When dope-sick, he could hardly speak. Got so run over by himself he'd collapse in his room and not come out for days. Emerge fragile, rebroken, sunless and a shade of his former. Hair curled into tight ringlets. Too-tight jeans and a penchant for black shirts.

Beat him silly with a pipe and laughed and laughed, but not callously, not hideously, almost mercifully. Blood was all over the walls, the bags of clothes, the door, dripping down like a cheap horror flick, life imitating art imitating love at its best. She forgave and forgave and took his legs out from under him on the stairs one day. "He had it comin," she said. Couldn't disagree there. He rarely retaliated, but when he did it was bad. Showed me her hip where he'd slashed her with a sharp piece of scrap metal. "But I got him good," she said. "It's just how we say good morning."

When the truth about his past and the
sexual interference conviction came out, he
cut lengthwise up the arm from the wrist
and went into the shower to finish the job.
Petri found him because the blood was
flowing into the hallway like a river from
Hades. He was out of the hospital and back
home in thirty-two hours. Yes I counted.

but listen gary

but listen gary the clouds close to the earth with wild pulling madness
but listen gary every morning is like this
but gary sometimes the hunger
   can swallow me with the force of a moment
gary the flies are circling in a swift column playing in the downdraft
   of an electric ceiling fan it looks like a lot of fun
but listen gary he stepped out of the doorway so suddenly his head
   mostly bald wrinkly tobaccoed and timecut roundnosed and sharpjawed
   i was a little startled you would've been too so early in the morning
but listen gary nobody asked me how i felt about it
listen she took the corner too fast her nice wheels were squeaking off
   the old cobblestone she was obviously trying to get somewhere and
   somewhere was obviously getting to her
but listen gary doesn't your mouth feel dry and bottlenecked
   sometimes like a thimble capping a well so much waiting to come
   out but nothing really fits
gary the waterfall roared and all of a sudden the molecules were just
   hanging there in mid-air
but gary i'm trying to hold back
but listen gary someday i'll die and i wanna be cremated and scattered
   into the sea i want to be fish food you will die too the sun will still
   come up the next whether we're here or not but i'm moving
   through the streets and the trees and the wind and the
   streets and the trees and the wind are moving through me
listen i counted the windows on the building across the street there
   are thirty-seven how come because its so symmetrical am i losing it
but listen gary the water is dripping from the ceiling so slowly filling
   the room i am building an ark out of these bones i had lying
   around
gary the gate is closing medusa is watching go through with your eyes
   closed
but listen we are heading for the pass
                     heading for the pass
but listen gary the temple erupted right there in the middle of the

woods and the snakes crawled out of the stones
but listen gary i swore i saw you in a crowd just yesterday
but sisyphus is in the eternal stairwell the dawn is crawling up his
spine
but gary desnos and his imagination are being deported again and
again and again
gary everyone should be astonished at the world
but listen gary i sat on the church roof listening to the hymns and the
smoke and the angels head up into the doomed starry vault
nothing really came of it
listen i can't even understand what happens to my heart or body
when she takes her clothes off how can i understand the galaxy or
a concept of eternity or art or even this sentence
but listen gary in my head i'm on the prow of a fast-sinking ship what
does that mean tell me
but who told you you had the right to do that i don't think it should
be up to you
listen gary sometimes i like to just sit and do nothing some people say
this is a waste of time but i know better
but is there really a library in the sky where every book has already
been written and a big wheel of fortune and is there destiny and
have we already lived a couple of times and when do i get to
choose and when will i find out for sure
gary i just wanted my wallet back i didn't expect all that dirt and
blood in my face
but listen there is a way that even shit can look pretty
gary the face of the wall looked like the blood of ten thousand
martyrs
but last night i screamed at the bottom of my lungs into an empty
orchestral hall the sound went nowhere and the lights were not on
listen do you think you have a doppelgänger
but listen gary what is the point of all this talking and talking and
talking and talking
gary the winch fit into a pulley which was rigged to a crane which
they used to lift behemoths right out of the water

but the world makes me afraid of a lot of things and the fear
　　sometimes knots me up into a fist and that fist wants to lash out at
　　the world and bash it to pieces what do you suggest that i do about
　　it don't say just meditate or i'll punch you in the face
but listen gary when he told me i collapsed wailing on the sidewalk
　　like a drunk now there's irony for you
listen the gas main burst open and the whole city smelled like doom
　　but to be fair doom was on my mind
gary i think suicide is always an option but that doesn't mean i have
　　to like it
but the force of the pillars holding up the ceiling holding up the walls
　　and building was always astounding
but listen gary i don't believe in angels or devils or any of that crap so
　　where are you now i can't picture it even though i've been told i
　　have a lovely imagination
but in the dream we were on the starboard and you were pointing out
　　the geometry of the island approaching and describing its
　　importance in shaping shipping lanes and the terrible shipwrecks
　　that happened there but in the end i woke up the same and you
　　were still dead
but gary where will i find the answers to jeopardy now
listen the process fit into the question and vice versa, but form and
　　function wanted nothing to do with it
gary i purged all those things from my mind but i'm not sure what's
　　left
but gary i might have changed my name too i understand the need
　　for becoming something new maybe now more than ever
but listen gary i remember you told me how you made a fortune
　　fishing golf balls out of the water traps and selling them back to
　　the golfers though you were never much of an entrepeneur what
　　an ingenious idea
listen i remember the hawk swooping down and tearing a small hole
　　in his head man that must have hurt but all i could think of was
　　that that was your favourite bird
gary please take away my wisdom and my categories

but listen gary there is no space in my head for anger anymore but it's
   there anyways and i can't make it leave do you have any
   suggestions
but most things on the radio sound like wilted broccoli i know you
   would agree
but listen gary there is desire and terrible beauty and water and grace
   and couldn't you find one reason for hanging around

in an 8 x 10 room in meccan city

out of order
a fire escape
                    i couldn't sense the non-emergency more if it
                    hit me with a truck

i reached into my pocket and took out a knife
and cut off my timing
      sweat it out took forever

"feels like your body and brain are melting apart"
i fought the law and the law always won

                                              jail
                                              jail
                                           vacant
                                         hospital
                                              jail
                                              jail
                                           vacant
                                          missing
                                              jail
                                              jail
                                           vacant
                                              jail
                                              jail
                                         hospital
                                           vacant
                                          unknown
                                              jail
                                         hospital
                                              jail

57

in my hand i held a copy of the original
the signature was illegible

indifferently hostile
hostile to indifference

i went from street to street to street to place to place to place
only more and no never no nothing else
it tasted like greenhouse, like

what to devour
what to fulminate, dissent, process, incarcerate, repeat
what to refuse
what to see as medicine, what not
what victory in the day-to-day
what to glean from time
what to extract from a pretty girl in a black dress who won't talk to me
what reward
what price freedom
what to leave for poison
what to visualize
what to presume as "unwanted"
what to steal, to beg
what to say
what to yield
what to discredit, incriminate, capitulate
what to gutter
what to scalp, poach, strip, recycle
what to spill
what to divulge
what to label as past expiry date but to eat anyway
what to debt, what to credit with what non-existent flow of non-existent cash
what to squeeze out, what to ignore
what to pick, peel, pustule or penniless
what to frame, bike or otherwise

what to ingest, spit, regurgitate
what to get me through the night
what to look through what window that won't open
what to consider rooftops with easy access and ten-storey drops
what to make of all this poorness living beside such richness
what to eat as food, only if to pretend
what to needle, what to vein, what to consider feeling better
what to baseline
what to redzone, what to avoid, what to consider worth the risk
what to be seen as something worth seeing, worth looking at
what to harass
what to file under "narcissistic," what to medicate, what to plant
what to find under and inside mattress, and on pillow, tiny blood stains and all
what to consider clothing
what to mythologize, NIMBY, eradicate, circumvent
what to hope for

a sense of things

      appearing composed, or uncomposed
      lines across face, crumpled sleep
        splashed across my desktop
        like a landscape, elbows askew

        mouth open and no teeth appearing
        nowhere breath not whistling
    what dreams of life

i am not able

> a time comes when silence is a betrayal
> when the quiet that curls in your throat
> must be immolated
> and the ashes coughed out
> to cover the earth in a noisy grey
> that it cannot wipe
> from its forehead

bloodlines

tripped the light fantastic, then just tripped
spit sunfire, echoed coins roman and cold
back to alert bay, to honesty's goodbye basin
hello bodega y quadra compass quandary

o lines frenetic, o lines unstraight and bloodwavering
crossing and recrossing and recrossing
cut through with territorial growing pains
o those pesky inhabitants, o silt of watered earth
trust me, there was no one there when we arrived
it was the cleanest of slates
trust me, it's still clean

what is there to see? what land is opened,
pleads furrowing, pleads own?
spoiled parallels, quadracepted and inverted
in tune with the local culture and economy

the prow cut through the water cleanly and left
a wide swath of memory and cartilage
we drank cups of international tea, bloodlines furrowed
across the soil
and the sand

merman

    bell sounds
    bite over
    dawn swallow
    tidemark
    merman
    x
    hissed
    salt wash
    horn and grimace
    the wash of the bay

    toxic in the city
    push of the sludge
    the underwater whirr of machinery
    cars on bridges
    yachts
    jet skis
    pulse of daylife and other
    clanks in the deeps

    rhythm
    rhythm
    rhythm
       in the constant water

    latent
    freighter cue
    ocean economy and engine
    under it all
    sleeps in the kelp
    the sun a long tunnel
    through the dark

off heading
will gone astray
turned something heavy
cold malicious
no other
and no taste of peace

a homemade sunrise

    beneath gravity and
    above time

    got a little boy in the trunk
    i joke
    shackled to ares at twenty-six thousand feet
    i try to think of something quiet
    but the propellers are deafening
    try to get my mind to stay
    suspended high
    over the salton sea
    i think of the expanse
    and the quiet

    [しかし平和はどこに…]

    but even in that
    quiet vastness
    even in that dust
    demons ghosts tears
    [i kept them private]
    jornada del muerto
    photographs of a four-ton dawn maker
    windy tarmac

    [しかし平和はどこに…]

    i can't help
    but imagine our contrails
    of ash and bone
    but i
    ain't got no quarrel with god
    we made peace a long time ago
    but now we
    make war
    we'll show him

what a sunrise
could really look like .
we'll harden the sands of time
into pearls of history
with one bright flash
cast some shadows
on that imperial sun
build a manhattan
over hiroshima
today nike of samothrace
comes diving with a little u-235
tucked behind her ear
fire and penance to
rend that veil
and show them
the divinity of hell

[しかし平和はどこに…]

i wonder if emily will
be proud of me
soft targets iknowbut
imnotsorryno
psych training and everything
ensured that
[they told us
they
toldus
to make a new
bloody sunrise
they even gave paul and me
little pistols
in case the boys
had a change of
heart]
close now throttle down

the beastly hum of the props
close now
no more blood
no more prisoners
buti
cant stop thinking
about those contrails
dragging a cloak of
ash and history
behind us
and then paul's
shouting at me
i know its time
i know
open the bomb-bay doors
that crazy rushing of air
0815 plus five seconds
we're all looking at each
other
nervousiknowbut
smile boys we're
making history here
paul gives the order
[the bombardier does his duty]
we all do
i mean
fuck the bhagavad gita
i just fly the plane
we'll get the cross if we pull this off
hey maybe two
i can't believe
it's falling away now

[しかし平和はどこに…]

smile boys we're
making history here

67

robert johnson sings the blues at the shangri-la, july 1937

like consumption
killing me by degrees
i can study rain

the list:
come on in my kitchen
walkin' blues
ramblin' on my mind
me and the devil blues
if i had possession over judgment day
love in vain
i believe i'll dust my broom
from four till late
crossroads blues
hell hound on my tail

she got a mortgage on my body, now,
and a lien on my soul

steps out on stage
that crazy evil eye
roamin' the jook joint
the other dead on me
sits down on the wooden chair
the smoke of the guitar strings
and the steel
curlin' from his cigarette
startin' off slow
you'd better come on in my kitchen
babe it going to be rainin' outdoors
foot tappin'
esu jumpin' behind the curtain
the whole joint in a silent cacophony

can't find my girl on philippines island
must be in ethiopia somewhere

his fingers spiderin' the chords
blues fallin' down like hail
right into the souls of the crowd
right into the eyes
of the kind-hearted woman
at a table by herself
pack of cards and a candle
little glass of whiskey
painted toes
red and black
red and black

i'm on get deep down in this connexion
hoo well deep tangling with your wires

no foolin
here is the crossroad
here is *connexion*
here is the where the paths
come together and go apart
can't get yourself unwound
can't find no solitude

i went to the crossroad baby
i looked east and west

partnered now for life
me and esu and this bottle
dancin' till my dusk
comes ringin' over the hills

red and black
red and black

untitled (maria's sister)

maria's sister
was raped by four
men before she was
killed in an alley
near fraser street

maria said she has to believe in god
because sometimes
that's all she has left
to hold on to

i said
i know what you mean
but i was lying

Mariner Janes was born in Victoria, British Columbia, and was raised in East Vancouver. His work has been published in *West Coast LINE* and in the chapbook *blueprint*. *The Monument Cycles* is his first book. While studying English literature at Simon Fraser University, he co-edited *iamb* magazine, a venue for new and emerging writers.

Janes is employed in Vancouver's Downtown Eastside and he aims to incorporate the multitude of voices he encounters there into his work, through found poetry, transcription and storytelling. He is currently working on a new collection of poetry and short stories.